T0182569

LOVE, FUTURE ME

Hope Ignites the Journey, Action Breaks the Impossible: Discover Your Spark Within These Pages – The Next Step Is Yours.

When a diagnosis of cancer is dropped on your life, it is, well, weird. The world shifts into slow-motion as you try your best to process what it all means. Meanwhile, as time feels distorted and surreal, your brain is running a mile a minute and cannot compute the world. Yes, the news knocked my knees out, but growing up a "weird kid" and into adulthood made me question all of life's possibilities. Besides, adversity and twists had become part of my story and I was done with letting others tell me what was possible in my life. Maybe this was just a new plot twist, spurring an awakening in my dreamer's story.

And what's with all these notes I found?

@ @wondervillestudios
f /wondervillestudios
in @beyondhopeproject
♪ @beyondhopeproject

LOVE, FUTURE ME

Notes to Open Hearts & Lift Spirits

JASON THARP

BEYOND HOPE PROJECT

Copyright © 2024 by Jason Tharp

Love, Future Me: Notes to Open the Heart and Life Spirits

www.beyondhopeproject.com
www.jasontharp.com

Published by Kayppin Media
Parkland, FL

Printed in China.

First Edition: October 2024
Disclaimer
This book is a work of non-fiction. Names, characters, businesses, places, events, locales, and incidents are either the products of the author's imagination or used in a fictitious manner. Any resemblance to actual persons, living or dead, or actual events is purely coincidental.

Library of Congress Cataloging-in-Publication Data
Tharp, Jason.
Love, Future Me: Notes to Open the Heart and Life Spirits / Jason Tharp
pages cm
Includes bibliographical refernces
1. Self-help. 2. Personal growth. 3. Inspiration. I. Title.

K KAYPPIN

Parkland, FL

ISBN 978-1-938447-98-3
LCCN 2023951939

Cover Design by Jason Tharp
Book Layout by Jason Tharp, Wonderville Studios, LLC
Set in Adobe Caslon and Gotham

To all past versions of me,

I forgive you. I know now that you were
doing the best you could with what you
knew about yourself at that time.
You're doing fine. Keep evolving.

Love,
Future Me

On July 12, 2021, an awakening began.
I wasn't looking for it. Or was I?

Welcome to Our Shared Journey:

Dive deep with me, embrace each
word, and remember – our path to
possibility starts right here, within
these pages and within you.

I hope you find a way to work these messages of affirmation and power into your daily practice. We all strive for perfection and fall into its trap. We can forget that perfection is an illusion, fake, and a form of resistance drawing us away from our goals. Practice is the preparation for all the imperfect things that will go wrong in our lives.

You could just read straight through this book and highlight a few of your favorite notes. I've drawn out some, copied them into my journal, or shared their sentiments with friends. Perhaps you'll take a photo and share it on social media. I encourage you to come up with your notes and share those. (And if you do any of the above online, please tag me! It would be awesome to see how far the notes travel.)

While there's no real answer for how you should use this book, here's what I do know: This book found its way to you, and I think that's wonderful. Please honor that by showing up for yourself, doing the tough stuff, and treating yourself with loving compassion. Being a human is hard, but those of us who are willing to dare, to try, to love ourselves and accept our imperfections—that's who really transforms impossible ideas into daily possibilities.

Have fun with this book, enjoy it, share it, and even shed a tear. I know I have. And you are worth all the effort . . .

CONTENTS

DISCOVERY

- 15 -

CONFORMITY

- 37 -

SWEATPANTS

- 59 -

FAILING

- 83 -

AMBITION

- 107 -

REVEALED

- 129 -

UNPREDICTABLE

- 151 -

LOVE

- 175 -

HOPE

- 197 -

IMPOSSIBLE

- 201 -

DISCOVERY

Just breathe. That's the mantra I found myself reciting, over and over. But it wasn't providing the relief I desperately sought as I spiraled, feeling out of control, reaching for some semblance of stability. Then, seemingly out of the blue - it's curious how life unfolds - on one of my darkest days, in my quest for a glimmer of hope, I stumbled upon love notes. These were not ordinary notes, but heartfelt messages, written by myself, to myself.

I don't remember writing them, and I don't know why I abruptly stopped. I do know that I wrote them well over a year before the face off with my foe. I dated each one and signed it "Love, Future Me." Then I left them like tiny treasures to one day be discovered. In 2021, I found these treasures at the very moment in time when I was battling anxiety and in the midst of a battle for my life. How odd that I don't remember writing these, I thought. But I knew the brain is a mysterious being. And when I found the notes, I held onto them like they were a life raft. It was as if I had written notes predicting everything that was going to happen to me. But what's the point of questioning it? That's the cool thing about the universe: the surprises! The unexpected. It was weird but it was comforting, beautiful, and everything

I needed. At a time when I was plagued by anxiety, I found comfort in my own words.

This blew my mind! For far too long, I'd stopped listening to my own words, finding countless reasons why I felt unworthy, like an outcast, and becoming a master in the art of self-sabotage. Isn't it funny how we often uncover our greatest treasures hidden within our biggest fears? Maybe, I just happened to be looking in the right direction. I am so happy I did.

For the sake of context, the book you are about to read, leaf through, mark up, and share as you see fit is a collection of notes I wrote to myself for a handful of months in 2020, surrounded by vignettes of story. I encourage you to see yourself in my story and draw parallels to moments in your life. I now invite you to share these bits of advice—this personal world. In total transparency, I've fought sharing this for a long time. This is weird and incredibly personal, even by my standards. But I am a firm believer that even in our darkest storms, love is always present, waiting for us to see it and know that all will be okay, and that encourages me to share my story. I hope you find hope in these words.

Life.

It's what happens when
you're waiting for someone's
permission to live.

Guess we better start living?

Want to know the secret to all your dreams? It's your thoughts, your words, and your actions.

———————————

You can't see it now, but amazing
things are headed your way.
Be on the lookout for the signs.

———————————

Your plans might not always align
with the actual course of events.

The person that will 'save you' is
the person reading this.
No one else is coming.
You up to the task?

Isn't time strange?

We can't wait for it to arrive.

Then wonder where it went.

Wishing we had it back.

Only to realize it's here with us

right here, right now.

There's no promise of tomorrow,
and this day will never come back.
Therefore, it seems like a good day
to start living.

Stop it!

They are worrying about

their own junk!

Remember when you
used to imagine?
That was cool.

I get it; you need to hear it once more:

You are enough!

Will this be the time you'll listen?

Today, I want to be amazing!
I told myself this at least a
thousand times.
But on one thousand and
one, I finally listened.
Be amazing today.

Live for the moments that
take your breath away, just
don't forget to breathe.
After all, that moment was
made for you.

———————————

Drawing boundaries with family
and friends feels cruel.
Isn't it just as cruel to sacrifice
your emotional well-being?
You're worth it!

———————————

Your decisions are your
decisions. Letting others decide
for you will always leave you
feeling, well - decision-less.

You have buried treasures locked
inside of you. To unearth them,
you must have the courage to
take bold action.
'X' marks the spot.

Despite how you may feel right now... I think you're cool. Just wanted you to know that.

Yes, you can. That's it.

I get it; finding magic in your day is really hard. So were walking, talking, writing, and riding a bike, but you did those. Forget what your brain is telling you and live like a six-year-old.

At some point, you started to believe that coloring inside the lines was better. This built walls and bred self-loathing. By the way, don't crayons smell awesome!?

COMFORMITY

I was born to be a storyteller. It's always been my safe place. When I read Syd Hoff and Shel Silverstein for the first time, I saw myself in the pages of their books. They became my instant besties and forever owned a small piece of my heart. And we've never even met! Funny how authors, books, artists can do that, right? Around six years old, it was Hanna-Barbera who captured my creative imagination and taught me how to be an artist. My parents had bought this amazing piece of technology called a VCR. (Young people, Google it!) I would record my favorite cartoon, press pause on an image, cover the television screen with paper, and trace my favorite characters. This became my daily art lesson. During one of these lessons, my parents said something that would change it all: "You know people get paid to do that?"

I perked up. "What?" They explained: "To make cartoons. It's a job." Looking back now as a parent myself, I'm certain they said it while giving it very little thought. For me, that's all it took! In that instant, I gave my heart away to the promise of being a storyteller and making cartoons.

There was one small catch, though. Growing up in a small town that had lots of hard-working people but zero "cartoon makers"—at least none that I knew of—made my already negative self-image even more negative. It's easy for us to think there's something wrong with us when we strive to pursue a path no one around us is following. This is especially true when we're young and figuring ourselves out. School wasn't much fun, and I spent more time dodging insults than making friends. I remember asking myself many times, "I wonder what's wrong with me?" Each time added another brick in my future bunker of self-loathing. My teachers would have said I wasn't the best student. The problem wasn't that I didn't want to learn. I couldn't figure out how to control my overactive brain. I spent more time in the hall writing over and over "I will not talk in class," than I did learning about where periods and commas go. To this day, grammar is my nemesis. It wasn't only grammar and math that threw me for a loop, it was the idea of conformity. Everyone had to learn the same way, learn the same things, behave the same way. They had to be normal. I saw the world in colors and emotions. I felt like conformity drained all the color away and made up a language I couldn't speak, let alone understand. Recently I was curious and Googled "Who determines what is normal?" It turns out statistics determine "normal." Go figure! Most of the time numbers guide our lives, not personal experiences and not emotions. This was certainly a language I couldn't speak. This felt lonely and had me asking myself, was I always going to be a stranger in this this strange land?

"You're different from
everyone else; that's ok.
We used to let that stop us.
So glad we got over that!

Accept yourself for who
you are.
So we can accept others
for who they are.

Discover play,

Discover you!

Yes, it's that simple.

The stuff you're using to judge yourself might be something that someone else idolizes about you.

I know you're hesitant, wondering if
you really can pull it off. It's okay.
One day, you'll realize those
moments were when you were on
the right path.

Don't change who you are to belong.

Be who you are.

If you ask me, that's the best me to be.

Limited thinking generates
limited results. Instead,
imagine the possibilities!
I believe in you.

Other people's expectations for your
mission isn't your mission statement.
They'll adjust.

A dandelion will pop up anywhere—and even places they don't belong. They don't ask, they just do what they do and shine as beautifully as they can. When's the last time you did that?

Stop making goals based on
what is out of your control.
Instead, become the best
human possible, add value,
and empower others.
You'll find that your goals
naturally happen.

What if achieving your life's goals is letting go of the idea that it's in everyone else's control?
You got this!

Your sparkle is YOUR sparkle.
It wasn't meant for someone else.
Owning your magic begins with
accepting you are unique and
different!

I know you say there's nothing special
about you, but that's not true. You are
the only YOU. No one can do what
you do. That's a fact!

You've always been original.

Don't become a copy.

Growing up, all we saw were our
flaws and how we didn't fit in. We felt
shame, insecure, and full of self-doubt.
Then like magic, one day, you'll realize
your differences are the things that
will change your world.
You amazing weird-o!

You're a good person
and doing okay.

Do whatever you can
to let this sink in:
I feel free,
Not being them,
But being me!

Share your dreams with others. The right people will check in, let you borrow their magic, and cheer you on. The others, well, probably best they moved on anyway.

I remember writing the same story of our life, hoping the ending will change with each reading. One day, I finally changed what I was writing. Here's a perfect beginning: 'Once upon a time, I thought I couldn't do it, and I don't want to think like that anymore…

SWEATPANTS

Growing up, I never knew how to fit in. Early on, I would say the most awful things to myself. The real problem wasn't the harsh words I used, though they were bad; it was that I believed every word. I managed to mask it and play the part, being whatever everyone else wanted me to be. The question always lingered, "Why don't people understand me?" I knew I was kind-hearted, nice, and just wanted them to see me for who I was and appreciate me. I'd go to great lengths to please people—a habit I carried into adulthood. Now, through the beauty of hindsight, I understand their perception had nothing to do with me and everything to do with them. As a child, though, hindsight doesn't exist, and grace feels out of reach.

So, like many "weird" kids, I piled on the shame. It was here, I now realize, that I began to form another version of myself, a mask of sorts. Throughout middle school and high school, I did my best to blend in. I thought if I just went with the crowd, I'd be safe and left alone, and for the most part, I was. I'd gotten so accustomed to wearing different masks that I doubt anyone noticed my struggles. How I wish I could go back and reassure that kid that it will be okay one day and this experience would be invaluable. But I likely wouldn't have listened.

Art was my one constant. Whether it was pastels, paints, markers, pencils, clay, or collage, these creative outlets always welcomed me with open arms. They provided an unconditional love, an escape from the facade I had created, and perhaps a pathway toward the real me. Even now, I lose myself in the canvas of a blank page, though these days it's more likely to be on my iPad. The world is open to possibilities, only limited by imagination. With my boundless imagination, I pondered if I could create all the worlds I could dream up.

Not yet. And it wasn't because I couldn't dream them up, but because I was unprepared and petrified of what that might lead to. But one day? Yes, that's possible.

After high school, food became my coping mechanism, a temporary fix for long-term problems. It helped me escape everything I wanted to avoid. Eventually, I found myself weighing around 400lbs, drowning in a sea of shame and self-loathing. Yet through all of this, optimism always survived in me, and I'm not sure how that of all things thrived.

A minor incident with a pair of jeans was a turning point. My wife dried the one pair of jeans I owned, and they shrank. In frustration, I blamed her, but the truth is, I was stuck in a cycle of blaming others. Internally, a dam broke, and it came in the form of sweatpants—that's all I had left that would fit me.

At this point, I had hit rock bottom for the first time. Regretfully, I ignored the awakening. Looking back, I wish I had paid attention. My sweatpants and I made the decision to join the gym and reclaim our health. I took control, lost over one hundred and eighty pounds, all while still avoiding my true foe.

"Stop worrying about what others think.

Stop telling yourself you're worthless.

Stop lying to yourself–let's start there.

The bad stuff is just as much a part
of life as the good.
The bad just hurts a little bit more.

Today, let's commit to taking
the first step.
Tomorrow, we may have to
begin again, and that's ok.
Gotta start somewhere.

There will be wins, losses, mistakes,
and triumphs in your life.
Congrats, you're human.

Being a positive person doesn't
mean there won't be bad days.
Some days will just suck.

One day someone you know
may need to hear this:
I am thrilled you're here. If you or
someone you know is in crisis, PLEASE
call The National Suicide Prevention
Lifeline (1-800-273-TALK [8255])
24/7, or text 'HELLO' to 741741

Change may be scary, but so
is staying stuck.
I get that you're feeling
stuck right now.
Maybe it's time to change?

Love yourself enough to do
the stuff that sucks!

The story you want to live is waiting for

you to write it.

You don't need an invitation.

You wouldn't throw eggs at
your own car, right?
So why do it to your own
self-esteem?

Stop thinking you are making
stuff for everyone else.
Your job is to create from your joy.
The world is waiting for it!

Learning to love yourself is
hard, especially when you
can only see your flaws.
What if looking at those
flaws is exactly how you
learn to love yourself?

After reading this, close your eyes and take a deep breath. Think of a time when you felt the most free, feel it in your heart, and make the choice to live that feeling each day. At first it will be hard, but with practice, you'll feel it.

You will make mistakes.

Learn to forgive yourself.

Mistakes don't mean you can't be great.

Mistakes will make you great.

STOP! You are enough. You are strong. You are capable. You aren't perfect. You are trying your best. And yes, it may be hard to believe these things, especially if you're focused on all the reasons you aren't these things. It's OK being you right where you are right now.

What if instead of feeling like you're going nowhere, you realize that you may be ahead of schedule?

Sometimes I spent days, weeks, or even years waiting for the perfect time, and other times I just got after it and the perfect thing showed up. Coincidence?

Past storms are for learning,

not reliving.

Life is an adventure, live it!

Do you ever wonder why you keep getting the same thing over and over? Maybe, I don't know, try a new route?

Life can be challenging,

but you're tougher.

Embrace those challenges,

they make you stronger.

Believe in your strength.

FAILING

My passion for creation led me to art school. I immersed myself in it with the same determination a four-year-old exhibits towards a new toy. Innocently, I thought hard work could silence my negative self-talk, making it magically disappear. But, as I would discover, my issues weren't so easily left behind; they would have followed me even if I'd relocated to the moon.

In my junior year, with a baby on the way, I needed a job - and fast. I ventured into the corporate world, a realm unfamiliar to me. I come from a lineage of hard workers, yet corporate life was a foreign concept. It felt like being shot out of a cannon; I tackled it by leaning on my knack for working tirelessly, often trying to outwork others. However, I quickly realized this was a fast lane to burnout.

Despite having fun and creating some cool stuff in the corporate world, I still felt like an outsider, as if I never truly fit in. To self-soothe, I projected my insecurities and shortcomings onto others, feeling as though 'they' — whoever 'they' were — were against me.

I went for a run one evening at the end of my rope, filled with stress and emotionally exhausted. At this point in my young career, I was where I felt was the top. I was making way more than I ever imagined, traveled some, and my family was secure. I should have been happy, right? But I wasn't. Like most adults, I was climbing the ladder of life on a single mission to make more money to buy more stuff. I wondered, why had no one mentioned the trade-offs? I yearned to be a storyteller, to create worlds, to inspire people.

On that run, a realization hit me: sometimes, we have to trade our dreams for reality. An outsider might have simply seen a man on a run, but internally, my thoughts were in overdrive. It felt like a life-or-death race. Then, an unusual question popped into my head, "What would happen if I said 'NO' to everything an adult was supposed to say yes to, and 'YES' to everything a six-year-old would want?" Could this unconventional approach unlock my dream? I didn't have an answer, but I knew I was about to leave my job and set out on a mission to find out.

This decision led me into what I now endearingly refer to as 'the failing years.' I can say with absolute certainty, if you're blazing your own trail, brace yourself for some rough tumbles. It was a creative Mecca for me, and I crafted some truly cool stuff. But I was clueless about how to navigate success. I made blunders, damaged relationships, blamed everyone for my failures, and self-sabotaged at every turn. It was proof that even when you're pursuing your passion for the right reasons, if you don't embrace your internal self, the external world will show you the exit. Little did I know, my inner adversary was quietly reveling in my losses, patiently waiting for the right moment to shake my world.

Listen, you must bounce the ball to get

better at bouncing the ball.

Staying static isn't helpful.

Self-doubt has always held us up.

I need you to move.

You can do this!

Just a friendly reminder, not every day will be a great day.

I assumed I would fall,
but instead I flew.
Who would have
thought?!

You are struggling, but there will be better times, and you've done tough things before.

Focus energy towards what
you want to create.
We've spent too much energy
on what we don't want.
Remember, you are a creator.

I love you for showing up to
do this work.
It's really scary and hard, but
the upside is wonderful!

The path to success is often littered with periods of failure. Hang in there.

You're so busy trying to solve everyone else's problem, but don't realize by solving your problems you're helping others solve theirs.

I was so stuck looking for answers from the outside. In the end, all the answers were in me the whole time. Things that make you go, 'Hmm'.

Start with the simple things.

You are more than the bad
things you say to yourself.
I remember how hard it was to
start to love us.
It does get easier.

———————————

Friendly reminder, when good or bad
things happen for you, take a moment
and see what you've learned? And
how can it serve you? It's the direct
deposit into the Bank of You.
Make it rain.

———————————

You may not know this: most
of the stuff you are worrying
about won't really happen.
What a relief, huh!?

I hope something magical
happens for you today.
Something so amazing
it stops you dead in your
tracks and reminds you
how amazing life can be.

You realize that making mistakes
is part of change? You'll have many
missteps along the way. I know, it's
supposed to be perfect. Ha, don't be
silly, it will never be perfect.

When you're stuck, do you focus
on problems or solutions? The one
you focus on is the one you'll see.

One of the hardest things to do
is to take action when you know
something has run its course, and all
signs are pointing to "YES!"
Yeah, that's a tough one.

Just because you messed up doesn't
make you a mess-up.

We always worry about what people will think of us. It's probably best to let that go. They have the same junk kicking around in their head. Instead, let's challenge ourselves to be present and let the magic happen!

It may not feel like it,

but you have this.

Take a leap of faith, and you might
surprise yourself.
Trust your wings, you're meant to fly.

AMBITION

I was left staring into the terrifying abyss of a job search website at 2:30 am, flooded in fear and a sea of tears. The bank balance was dwindling, down to a mere $140, and I'd just received the call - the bank was foreclosing on my house. Each sob was a confirmation of failure and the terrifying prospect of working for someone else again. I had made a pact with myself when I left my last job – I was done working for anyone but me. But now, the reality was ruthlessly nudging me towards breaking that promise.

Amidst this chaos, I found solace in a delusion of survival fueled by blind ambition. I believed that if I dreamt it, it would happen. However, life isn't a movie script. You need a plan, action, and belief, and having just one or a few isn't enough. Optimism, my secret superpower, flew in to shake me out of my daze. Suddenly, my inner voice sounded weathered, assertive, and resolute. It posed a simple, poignant question: "What are you doing? Is this really how you're going to let it end?"

Propelled by a newfound defiance, I found a cheap flight and AirBNB in New York City. Armed with a slim credit balance of $400 and a series of meetings lined up, I began to write. Unburdened by the judgment of whether it was good or bad, I just wrote. Embracing my strength - drawing - and using it to compensate for my weaknesses, I stopped wasting energy on what I didn't want and started focusing on what I could create.

Publishers were drawn to my work, either due to its novelty or the raw passion that propelled it. I entered the ring with an unyielding "I won't be denied" attitude, and it worked. That trip, a temporary salve on the wounds of my life, provided much-needed relief.

As my books started to gain momentum, I visited schools, reaching out to the "weird" kids, those who were like me. I rode on the illusion of having tamed my inner critic, only to be pulled back to the harsh reality once I reached my car — a stark reminder of all the reasons I was inconsequential, a loser fooling no one. This made my foe very happy. It was cruel, but to me, it was normal. Why expect anything different when that's what you've always known?

You're doing great.

Even when you think you aren't!

Be present.

Making up stories isn't helpful.

No one is out to get you.

Focus, the world needs more of

what you have to offer.

Don't like what you see?
This helped me;
Take a deep breath and say,
"I'm the best me that I can
possibly be."

"That one time…"
Is a story of who we were, not
who we are now.
You've changed and that's good.

You don't need to compromise on a dream, but you may need to compromise on how it comes true. Amazing things come in many forms.

Under a microscope, the
biggest dreams are all made
up of tiny little steps.
Dang, guess you should stop
worrying so much.

Have you ever thought that
your timeline and the universe's
timeline may not match?
You could be early, but you're
never late!

If you stop to notice all of the
magical things you've already done,
you'd probably wouldn't feel so
overwhelmed with feeling you
haven't won.

Could it be that the inspiration
you are looking for is looking
for you also? Maybe you both
are looking in the wrong
direction… Dress up, stand out,
get noticed: let it know you are
ready for its arrival.

Sometimes you just need to carve
out time for that "thing" that lights
your passion. Your dream isn't dead,
you just stopped feeding it.

Did you know dreams and ideas are floating around you all the time? They are waiting for a shoulder to land on to become real. Are you open to it or busy worrying about all the things you aren't?

Dance even if you don't hear music.

Your bravery will draw others to you.

What if I told you that everything
you've been waiting for is just beyond
all the things you don't want to do?
Would you be willing to try then?

Sometimes the thing you think you
want is exactly what you shouldn't
have. It's the growth that comes
from chasing it you really need.

Your imagination is the quickest and shortest way from can't to can, from have not to have, and "wishing I had" to "I did it!"? Imagine it. Plan it. Do it.

What if you're seconds away from your big break and you just showed up ahead of schedule? Take a seat, breathe, maybe doodle a little.

Think about this: your "I can'ts" are
holding back your "I dids"

Practice makes perfect is false.
Practice is preparation for all the
imperfect things that will happen.

You need to do something just

for you, no one else!

REVEALED

On July 12, 2021, after enduring years of stress and self-loathing that could fill three lifetimes, my foe finally caught up with me. It happened while I was chatting with my son's basketball coach. Suddenly, the words I thought I was articulating weren't reaching my mouth. My next memory was of waking up with my phone buzzing, nestled in my lap, and his coach calling me back. He was inquiring about my wellbeing, explaining how he had attempted to contact me several times, given our conversation had ended abruptly as if I'd suddenly been submerged underwater. Perplexed, I responded, "Yeah. I'm good. Just fell asleep." I recognize in hindsight how odd this must have sounded.

It wasn't until I was walking down the hall from my studio to the bathroom that I noticed my shoes were missing from my feet. I remember being stumped and wondering where they were. In the bathroom, I noticed, with more confusion, that I had peed in my pants. As a grown man with no bladder issues, this situation left me utterly baffled! This incident later proved to be a crucial clue to understanding what had transpired. I did eventually locate my shoes, neatly stacked atop one another in the front loft of the building—an area I rarely visited.

Sorry to say, I drove myself home, making an awkward journey to the bathroom to shower and clean up. I knew something was wrong when I felt as if I was levitating in the shower. Luckily, by the time I made it downstairs, my wife decided it was time to head to Urgent Care. There, medical practitioners were just as puzzled as we were about what had occurred and sent me across the street to the emergency room for a CT scan.

I felt somewhat normal by this point, from what I can recall, and the scan wasn't too distressing. However, the doctor's subsequent announcement that a "shadow" had appeared on my results indicated that I wouldn't be going home just yet. I needed to wait for a bed at the hospital. If you're bewildered reading this, then I've successfully conveyed my confusion at the time. The doctor did bring me back to reality by stating, "Look, if I had a family member in this position, I would do the exact same thing!" Message received, doctor—I wasn't going anywhere.

Once a bed became available, we were transferred to the hospital, where I waited in another bed. My recollections here are blurry—I believed I was there for one day, but it was actually three. In the middle of the night on day two, after consuming a dreadful-tasting contrast solution, I was taken for an MRI, then returned to my room to wait, hungry and trying to make sense of it all.

Eventually, a young doctor appeared and asked, "Did anyone share your results with you?" We swiftly responded, "No." They pulled up the file on the computer and said, "It looks like a high-grade glioma. Someone will be in to speak with you shortly." And with that, they departed, leaving us wondering what a high-grade glioma was. After a couple of hours, I made a critical error. I demanded, "Give me my phone, please," less of a request, more of a directive. Why I thought it was a good idea to consult Dr. Google, I'll never know, but the prognosis was not encouraging.

Oh, the peeing my pants incident, it turns out that this is a side effect of someone having a complex partial seizure. As for the foe I'd been avoiding all my life, it wasn't all the individuals I had blamed, shamed, been hurt by, or hurt for my problems. The reality hit me like a bolt of lightning—it was me. As I was soon to realize, I was the problem all along.

Everyone you're blaming
things on isn't at fault.
It's you, it sucks and doesn't
feel good, but it's true.

Get busy living, 'cause
you're already dying.
From the second you
were born.

Surrender to the next
stage of your evolution.
It used to scare you,
but it saved you.

I forgive you.
You were doing the best you
could at the time.
We all make mistakes, take it
easy on yourself.

Funny thing is: I was the
problem all along.
Unreal how much time
I wasted looking for
something to blame.

I wish I had known how much of
a problem I was all along.
Maybe I would have addressed
things sooner.
Learn from my mistakes.

Sometimes making a HUGE
impact isn't moving a mountain
for someone. It's as easy as saying,
'Here's a book, it helped me feel,
and I hope it helps you.' The
magic is showing up, listening,
and offering a lifeline. We all can
use a hand from time to time.
You're so badass!

I'm my favorite person, and I didn't
even like us at first.
Crazy how much all that self-work
you're afraid of worked.

I spent so much time trying to
outrun myself before I sat down
and got to know myself.
You'll love what you find out.

Being a light in the storm for someone doesn't mean you have to be what they want. It means becoming everything you wished you were. Others will find your story inspiring, and it will help guide them out of their dark space.

Somewhere along the line we
stopped believing in our dreams.
Are you ready to re-discover
your dreams?
I'm waiting for you.

Today, I will take a chance on myself.
I remember feeling this, and thought
you may need the reminder!
It's okay to read it again.

Sometimes letting go of those who aren't helping you be the "best you" is the best thing you can do. It is a painful but a necessary step in your growth. You've got to love yourself.

The time has come for us to move
from can't to can. Self-doubt doesn't
serve you and never will. The real
question is: Are you ready?
I'm your biggest yaysayer.

When you're mining the gems in your life, remember this: What's the point of calling them "hidden gems" if they aren't hidden?

Don't let all your past people try
to rewrite your future.

Things in your past did happen.
Now, accept that it doesn't define
your future. Ask, do I want to stay
the same or do I want it to change?

You know that real impact
you want to make in your life?
Remember why you want to
start in the first place.

Ever notice right when you are
about to have a breakthrough, that
a challenge happens?
What if it's the universe saying,
"Dream bigger!"

UNPREDICTABLE

As it turns out, a high-grade glioma is far from a minor issue; it's like super-cancer. Following the discovery of my unwelcome brain buddy, I promptly underwent surgery, and thanks to a highly skilled surgeon, the operation seemed successful. Not being one to prolong a hospital stay, I found my strength rapidly returning after surgery and made it home in just two days.

As you might imagine, there is a tremendous amount of anxiety when you're waiting for your first doctor visit after surgery. Did they get all the cancer out? The waiting feels like forever, especially because you, the patient, are sitting in the proverbial dark with no idea what that thing was that they removed from your body. It especially took a mental toll on me because the stories I always told myself during moments of self-talk were horrible. Growing up, feeling different and unsupported, I'd say things to myself that would feed that narrative, such as "No one likes you!" or "You're a bad person and don't deserve good things." I'd then do things that would reinforce these negative beliefs. When I was diagnosed with cancer, it reminded me once again of how different I was, intensifying the feeling that I deserved the bad things happening to me.

After a few weeks the day finally arrived, and the doctor became the storyteller. They explained (horribly, I should add) that this chapter of my story would be titled Glioblastoma. They quoted statistics about what was considered normal for someone embarking on the journey I was on. It looked like a very short, unpleasant journey.

But you tell me what's normal and I'll turn in the opposite direction.

Let me pause here and clarify: I'm not saying to ignore your doctor or other experts. But I am asking you to give the following some thought: Doctors are experts on statistics, meds, and what's considered normal. They aren't, however, experts on you! You know who is an expert on you? YOU!

This is where the trouble with statistics comes in. They're numbers, they aren't you. Whether they're about a new miracle drug or a new disease, statistics generally track effectiveness, challenges, and trajectories. But these past statistics aren't your future prognosis, your lot in life, your defining thing. Statistics help us look ahead, but they don't predict the future. I believe we make our fate. As far as I was concerned, I was a 45-year-old male who had a successful surgery that removed the whole tumor. My case was my case, and it wasn't meant to fit into the same box as the thousands of other brain cancer cases. They weren't a measuring stick for my unpredictable future—and I certainly wasn't just going to accept their truth as my truth. This was a new beginning for me and other people were already trying to write my ending. Little did they know, I'd been telling stories my whole life, and I knew a lot could happen between "once upon a time" and "the end." Yes, it's completely possible they weren't capable of wrapping their normal way of thinking around my weird way of thinking, and that was okay. I'd been misunderstood my whole life.

"It's okay that you doubt
yourself sometimes.
Heck, I still do it from
time to time, I just stopped
letting it define me.

The path will show up.

I know you feel lost sometimes.

You gotta trust me on this one.

Who told you it was impossible?
They aren't in control of what
you can create.

I often wonder, why did it
take most of my life to get to
know the real me?
That whole time, it never
crossed my mind that I would
love myself as much as I do.
There's still time to learn
from my mistake.

I felt the most free when I stopped

being them and started being me.

You ready?

Our past isn't who we are.
Self-healing is real, and
this is all temporary.
Forgive yourself, you were
doing the best you could at
the time.

A diagnosis isn't the end,
it could be the beginning.

If you're writing the story
of your life, why not write
a helpful one?
I believe in you.

You will always find the right
people at the right time.
You just need to be looking in
the right places.

Somewhere between
desperation and devastation,
I found my determination.

Have you ever noticed how
things seem impossible...
until they aren't?

———————————

Have you ever wondered if today's
loss might be tomorrow's win?

———————————

Any pain that you may
go through is temporary.
Your growth from it will be
permanent. Even when it
doesn't feel like it.
Hang in there.

Storms can show up out of nowhere
and demolish all our hopes and
dreams. I remember it feeling like
it was going on for days, weeks, and
even years! I was so focused on the
storm, and missed that above it all
the sun was up there being all sunny.
Even the worst storms have to end.

Just remember, no happy ending began with, 'Once upon a time, there was a person who had zero problems...' What should we write today?

What if all the amazing things
you want to do are behind all the
goodness you're afraid to share?

———————

If you're reading this...
Remember that dreams don't have
deadlines. It's never too late to chase
what sets your soul on fire.
I believe in you!

———————

Our greatest growth will come out
of our deepest struggles.
Just keep climbing!

I knew inspiring people would make me happy, but happiness didn't happen until I did less thinking and more doing.

Remember when that good time passed? Remember when that horrible time finally ended? I guess good and bad times move on. Probably shouldn't define our future lives by the current 'time' we are in, huh?

That thing you've been thinking about trying. Maybe you should come up with a plan and start? You know you don't need to know all the answers to try, right? Everything BIG started with tiny steps forward.

LOVE

I left that first office visit knowing two things: One, this doctor can stay here where the normal ones hang out because I'm heading over to where the weird ones hang. I fired them because there would be no place for them on this team—on my team. Because when you're planning to turn what others determine impossible into something possible you must surround yourself with people who will encourage and believe in you. My journey of healing began when I realized that I had to take charge of my own life. Although hope from others can be incredibly powerful, there comes a time when you have to rely on yourself and take action. As a cancer patient, I learned the importance of advocating for myself—asking questions, conducting research, and making decisions best suited for my life. After all, I'm the one living it; I'm the expert on me.

As a child, I often felt different, and my cancer diagnosis only intensified that feeling. It dawned on me that those childhood struggles didn't make me weaker; they'd actually created my greatest strengths as an adult. Embracing my unique quirks and differences empowered me to face this new challenge head-on and gave me resilience. And finding new doctors who aligned with my determination to forge my own path proved invaluable. In this challenging time, I discovered the strength to direct my own destiny instead of following the prescribed path.

After that first visit, I felt confident and determined to heal— to become healthy, whole, and safe. But when we want to do hard things, the universe test us. It's as if it asks, "You can do this—but how bad do you want it?"

So, for the first time in my life, I braced myself to face my most formidable adversary—myself.

For much of my life, I projected my desires onto the world, never truly believing I was deserving of them. I constructed multiple versions of me, and at this moment, it felt as if I had been guiding two younger versions of myself through life.

In my right hand, I held the noisy me, filled with fear and incredibly loud. He demanded my attention for an extended period. In my left hand, I held love, along with all my hopes and dreams. This quieter version represented all the beauty and positivity I aspired to in my life, and unfortunately, I took this one for granted.

As I tried to appease the rowdy one, I inadvertently let love slip away. I kept feeding the loud child all the tales he wanted, thereby enabling his behavior. The more he clamored, the more I sought to manifest his desires. Then, I found myself alone, truly seeing myself for the first time, as if facing my own reflection in a proverbial mirror.

Exhausted by fear, weary of its illusions and lies—so many lies—I yearned for grace, a respite, for myself. I longed to reclaim my time, but I realized that this too was an illusion. Just as I thought I had lost love forever, I discovered that love had been quietly guiding me all along, leaving breadcrumbs for me to follow.

Upon encountering the quieter version of myself, his response was simple, "Hi, where have you been? I've been waiting for you." Taking his hand again, I found a new path leading back to me. In that moment, I recognized that armed with hope, I had the power to transform the impossible into possible.

"I LOVE MYSELF!
It can be the hardest
thing to say.
Totally worth it!

You are good enough to love.

Read that a few more times.

One day, you'll believe it.

Sometimes,

it will take all our heart

just to say,

'I really love me, and I

think I'll stay this way.'

Being self-loving isn't
being selfish.
We all have to learn to
love ourselves first.

Wonder opens the
door to be yourself.
Magic happens when
you love yourself.
Destiny happens when
you let go.

It was easy asking lots of
questions of myself.
It was hard to shut up and
listen for the answer.
Funny the solution is always
hidden in the hard stuff, huh?

Perfection is a complete lie.
The growth you're looking for
lives in your imperfections.
Stop trying to be perfect for
imperfect people.

Look up. Find three things to be
grateful for right now.
This is how you'll change your life.

It's really good to see you.

I've always known you're amazing.

Keep going.

No matter how hard you try, you're
never gonna outrun your fears.
Besides, your fears are where the
real growth happens.

Forgiveness, while it may not
be easy, will set you free.
Those you might resent are
moving on with their lives.
Maybe it's time for you to do
the same?

When I was left to my own devices, I would tell myself the worst things. I judged myself like I was the first person to ever mess up. Then one day I realized that people make mistakes all of the time, and I'll make more. It's all in making sure you learn from the mistakes that count.

What if everything you've been waiting for is on the other side of all the bad things you're focused on?

Perfection is a trap. It will feel
so close, and do everything to
lure you into its web. Be careful!
It will leave you stuck, waiting,
and not doing a dang thing.
Besides, you're not perfect,
you're human.

When you find yourself with
too much love in your heart,
put it on a string and share it
with the world.

Starting small is perfectly
fine. Be consistent.
With consistency comes
confidence, and when
problems arise you'll say,
'been there, done that!'
Everyone starts somewhere.

When you think all is lost,
you are alone, and you are
feeling completely worthless.
I am still here waiting and
hoping you'll see me.
Look for me.

It's fun to watch you do the
'impossible'.
Happy you finally realized
how awesome you are.

What if forgiveness, joy, sadness, fear, bravery, and all other good and bad emotions are undercover opportunities reminding us to experience our lives and grow.

HOPE

As I bring this narrative to a close, the paramount lesson is this: traversing this journey alone is impossible. It requires an incredibly diverse team. Every single person who crosses your path plays their part, including the ones who might have seemed not so good at the time. Admittedly, there were many times when I've felt completely alone, as though I was walking an empty path. Instead of tearing down the walls, I unknowingly built others, thinking I was protecting myself. These walls were nothing but illusions, fed by my insecurities, leaving me anchored in the familiar past and fearful of stepping into the unknown future.

The world can be loud, filled with distractions that blind us from seeing anything other than our current situation. Sometimes, we may even find peace in those who echo our insecurities, using their affirmation as validation. However, I've learned that we're never as alone as we think, and we all possess the power to change, regardless of our circumstances.

The saying that "hurt people hurt people" is one I initially dismissed as not applying to my situation. Recognizing yourself as a hurt person is hard to come to terms with, especially when hurt is all you've known. While this may be true it doesn't need to continue to be they way you measure your life. Take back your power. I can't emphasize enough the importance of knowing that you have control of situations that seem out of your control. As the creator of your life, you can choose your reaction, both emotionally and physically, to any situation. We cannot control how others react to our truth; we must hold true to our values, and that can be tough when being brave for yourself is so new. It takes a lot of trust in the unknown, but listen to that small voice; it sometimes knows better—after all, it is you.

I wish for everyone who reads this book or encounters my content online to identify with my story. My hope is that my reflections can create a connection that might prevent someone from inflicting further hurt on themselves or others. We're all hurting enough already.

For far too long, I felt like people were out to get me. Failing to recognize I was the common denominator. Think about it for a moment and how it applies to your life. How often do you choose to blame others, hold grudges, or participate in worthless gossip of those who "got you"? I am so grateful for the clarity that my brain buddy brought to me about this. Often, I have thought about how awesome it would be to have the ability to turn back time (which I know is impossible). I'd assure my past self that the world isn't as daunting as it seems.

Who knows? Maybe I can catch you before it's too late. Love is always present, and fear is close by as well. Sometimes, it's a simple shift in our gaze that will open our world to the joy we seek.

In the end, I hope my words bring some encouragement and the assurance that we are never truly alone. The world can be a scary place, but it is also full of promise. The only limit to the possibilities resides in you. And no matter what, never forget, we're all in this together.

What seems impossible
today can become possible
tomorrow. Open the door
when hope arrives, trust it, and
the path will become clear.
The power is in your hands.

IMPOSSIBLE

Not liking myself had been my path for so long, but I found love and a new path. I am driven to tell my story in hopes that others feel seen, not alone, and to assure them that it's never too late. Please know, perfection is a trap, and practice doesn't make perfect; practice is preparation for all the beautiful imperfections that will happen in your life.

Let me be clear: even with love firmly in my hand, it didn't mean that the fear went away. I learned through lots of practice how to not let fear take the lead. It's through my imperfections and perseverance that I have grown, evolved, learned to forgive, and accept and love myself for who I am.

Remember, hope is an amazing drug. It's the first step necessary to turn the impossible into the possible. Taking action is the crucial next step after finding hope. Combining hope with measurable action propels you towards achieving your 'impossible.' Never forget, love is always present, waiting to be acknowledged. All we need is a clearer perspective to see it, for love is there every moment of every day, waiting for you.

You possess the power to accomplish more than you can imagine. My journey, from battling cancer to reflecting on my childhood, has opened my door of wonder and allowed love to flood in. After my diagnosis, remission became my new 'impossible.' Technically, there's no such thing as remission when it comes to my diagnosis, but again, I'm not much for others' definitions. So on December 22, 2022, after well over a year of completely clear scans, I asked my amazing doctor if we can call this remission yet. He agreed that for me, yes. Mission Remission accomplished, but the work is never done.

Currently, I'm defying the odds with an undetectable tumor, having made significant changes to my diet and lifestyle. Looking back at my younger self, I can't help but think about what I would say to him. The struggles I faced have fueled and saved me while making me the person I am today, and I hope sharing my story can inspire others to do the same.

In closing, although we may not know each other, I want you to know you're doing great. Life can be tough and unpredictable, but you've overcome challenges before. Keep going!

Love,
Present Me :)

I'VE LEARNED, I'VE GROWN, AND NOW IT'S TIME TO BRING IT ALL INTO THE PRESENT. LET'S SEE WHAT TODAY BRINGS...

BEYOND HOPE PROJECT™

H.O.P.E. is a Strategy™

At Beyond Hope Project, we embrace the transformative power of beginnings. Our mission is to help you find your starting line and then guide you back to the path when you lose your way. We light the way for your journey, not dictating it, empowering you to transform aspirations into achievements through hope.

Our ethos is rooted in the profound impact of hope— it ignites dreams and sustains them, even in the face of challenges. Our offerings, infused with hope, aim to inspire and support, guiding you back to your path whenever you stumble.

We value transparency and authenticity, providing real tools for genuine journeys. Our goal is to add more hope and joy to the world than we take, impacting lives and reshaping futures.

Join us in our journey of transformation, powered by hope and the belief in limitless potential. Beyond Hope Project was born from Jason's life-changing glioblastoma diagnosis. His own journey through cancer and introspection revealed a need among adults for hope and resources. Defying odds, Jason's experience inspired the founding of Beyond Hope Project, a movement turning today's impossibilities into tomorrow's realities.

www.beyondhopeproject.com

Find Jason on all the socials by simply searching his name.

ABOUT JASON

Jason Tharp is a celebrated author, illustrator, and motivational speaker known for his fervent advocacy of individuality and self-acceptance. Rising above challenges including intense perfectionism, financial hardship, obesity, and a harrowing brain cancer diagnosis, Jason draws from these profound experiences to offer a fresh and invigorating perspective on life and self-betterment. With his dynamic illustrations, captivating narrative approach, and invaluable life insights, he stands as a testament to positivity and resilience, motivating countless individuals to face their fears and cherish their distinctiveness. He passionately promotes the ideas of redefining success, viewing imperfections as assets, shattering perceived limitations, and stepping forward with unwavering courage and self-compassion. Dive deeper into Jason's inspirational journey by visiting:
www.jasontharp.com.

OTHER BOOKS BY JASON

Jason's books, crafted from the stories he longed for as a child, carry a powerful message: embracing uniqueness is a special gift. His writings inspire children to find magic in their own stories, celebrating the beauty of being different. As Jason expands his mission to adult readers, his passion for hope and transformation shines through, guiding all ages on a journey of self-discovery and acceptance. This showcase offers just a glimpse; for the full library, scan this QR code:

ACKNOWLEDGEMENTS

I am so deeply thankful to so many people. My wife and rock, Becky, thank you for always being there for me, showing such patience while I was figuring out who I was, and accepting my quirks and imperfections. Thanks for letting me know that it's okay to be me. Thank you for logging countless walking miles, talking me off the ledge when anxiety took over, and spending time with me when I was too scared to face myself. Your belief in my big, lofty dreams means the world to me.

Dylan and Logan, you guys have no idea how much joy you've brought into my life. You are, hands down, the best thing I've ever done.

Thanks to all the medical professionals whom I've met, and special thanks to Dr. Fleming for being such an amazing surgeon, and Dr. Raval for saving my life with a simple phone call. Dharma, my friend, you've got a permanent place in my heart. Dr. Giglio, you're the best co-captain I could ever ask for on this healing journey. And to the doctor whom I won't name, thank you for knocking down the wall that led me to find myself.

A huge thanks to everyone who's been part of my journey. Doesn't matter whether it was a good part or a not-so-good part, you all helped me become the person I am today. For that, thank you. And I hope you get the chance to meet this version of me - I promise, it's an upgrade.

As for the future, I'm so ready to meet you. But right now, I'm going to chill out and enjoy this moment.